MW00474151

Not your average

40TH BIRTHDAY PARTY Guest Book

Copyright © 2018 by Julie Gilbert

All rights reserved. This book or any portion thereof
may not be reproduced or used in any manner whatsoever
without the express written permission of the author.

www.FromtheRookery.com

Welcome to my Birthday

Flip to any page and dive in. Doodle, draw and leave a comment!

Thank you!

Guest Self Portraits

Don't forget to sign your art!

Guest Self Portraits

HAPPY BIRTH DAY

I just wanted to say...

Bucket list suggestions

Bucket list
suggestions

leaf

a message

you can doodle here!

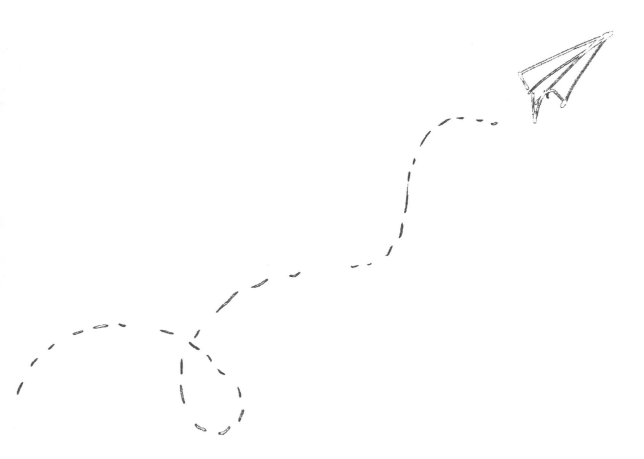

Reasons

you're a star!

Share your advice

for the future

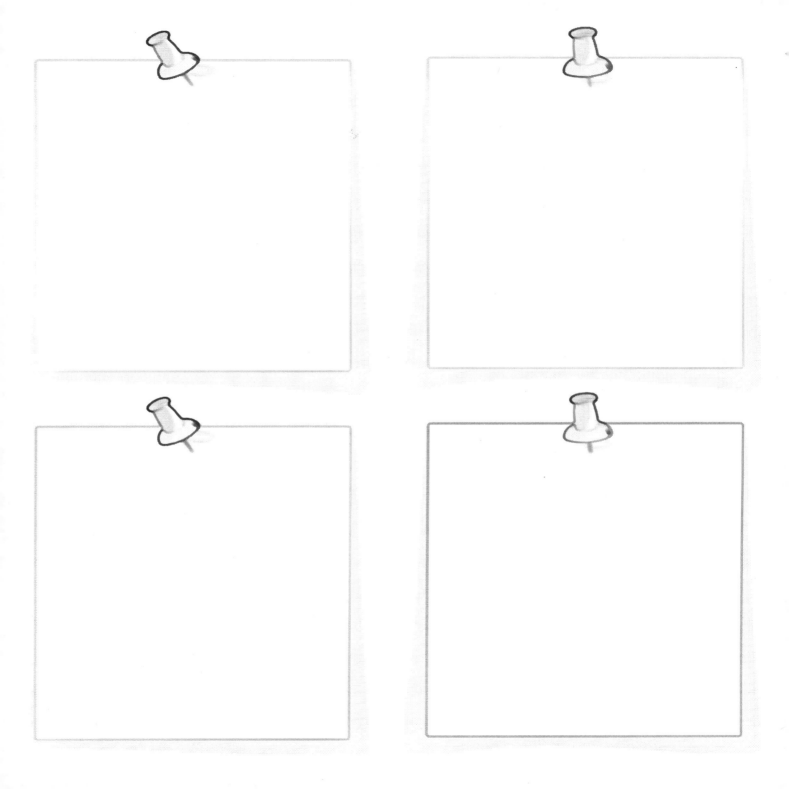

Thank you for

your memories

Birthday

Wishes

Birthday Wishes

Share a secret..

Guest creativity page

draw, write, doodle!

Happy Birthday

I just wanted to say....

Guest Artwork

Don't forget to sign your art!

Bucket list
suggestions

Bucket list
suggestions

leaf

you can doodle here!

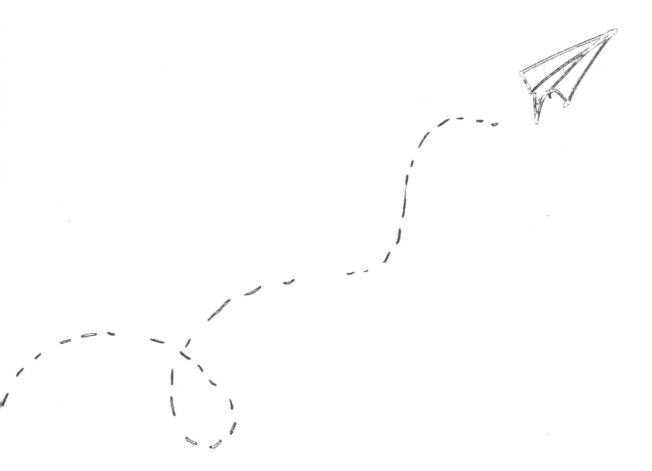

Reasons

you're a star!

Thank you for

your memories

Birthday

Wishes

Guest creativity page

draw, write, doodle!

Guest Self Portraits

I just wanted to say....

Share your advice

for the future

Birthday Wishes

leaf

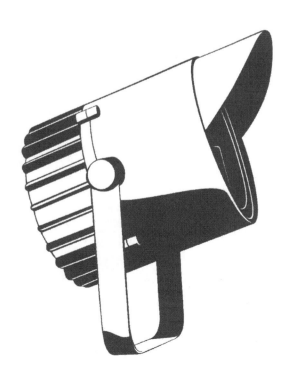

Event Highlights

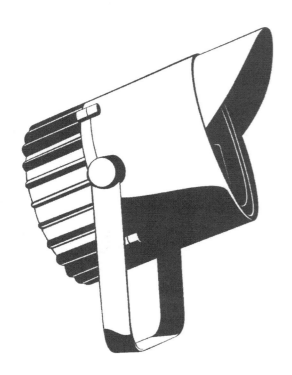

Event Highlights

Event menu:

Guest list:

_____

_____

_____

_____

_____

_____

_____

_____

_____

_____

_____

_____

_____

_____

_____

_____

_____

_____

_____

_____

_____

_____

Guest list:

_____   _____

_____   _____

_____   _____

_____   _____

_____   _____

_____   _____

_____   _____

_____   _____

_____   _____

_____   _____

_____   _____

_____   _____

Guest list:

_____

_____

_____

_____

_____

_____

_____

_____

_____

_____

_____

_____

Guest list:

_____

_____

_____

_____

_____

_____

_____

_____

_____

_____

_____

_____

_____

_____

_____

_____

_____

_____

_____

_____

_____

_____

Guest list:

_____

_____

_____

_____

_____

_____

_____

_____

_____

_____

_____

_____

Guest list:

_____

_____

_____

_____

_____

_____

_____

_____

_____

_____

_____

_____

Add your photos here!

Add your
photos
here!

Add your
photos
here!

Add your
photos
here!

Add your
photos here!

Add your photos here!

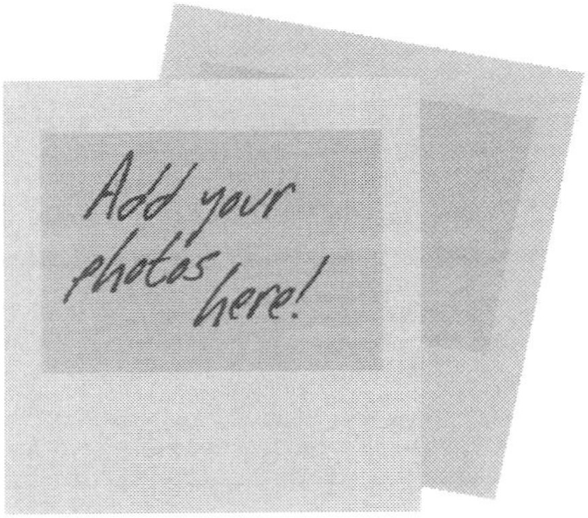
Add your
photos here!

Add your
photos
here!

Add your
photos
here!

Add your
photos here!

Gift Log

Guest	Gift	Thanks

Gift Log

Guest	Gift	Thanks

Gift Log

Guest	Gift	Thanks

Gift Log

Guest	Gift	Thanks

Gift Log

Guest	Gift	Thanks

Gift Log

Guest	Gift	Thanks

85582676R00069

Made in the USA
San Bernardino, CA
21 August 2018